JUNE

Ellen Jackson

Illustrated by Kay Life

📖 Charlesbridge

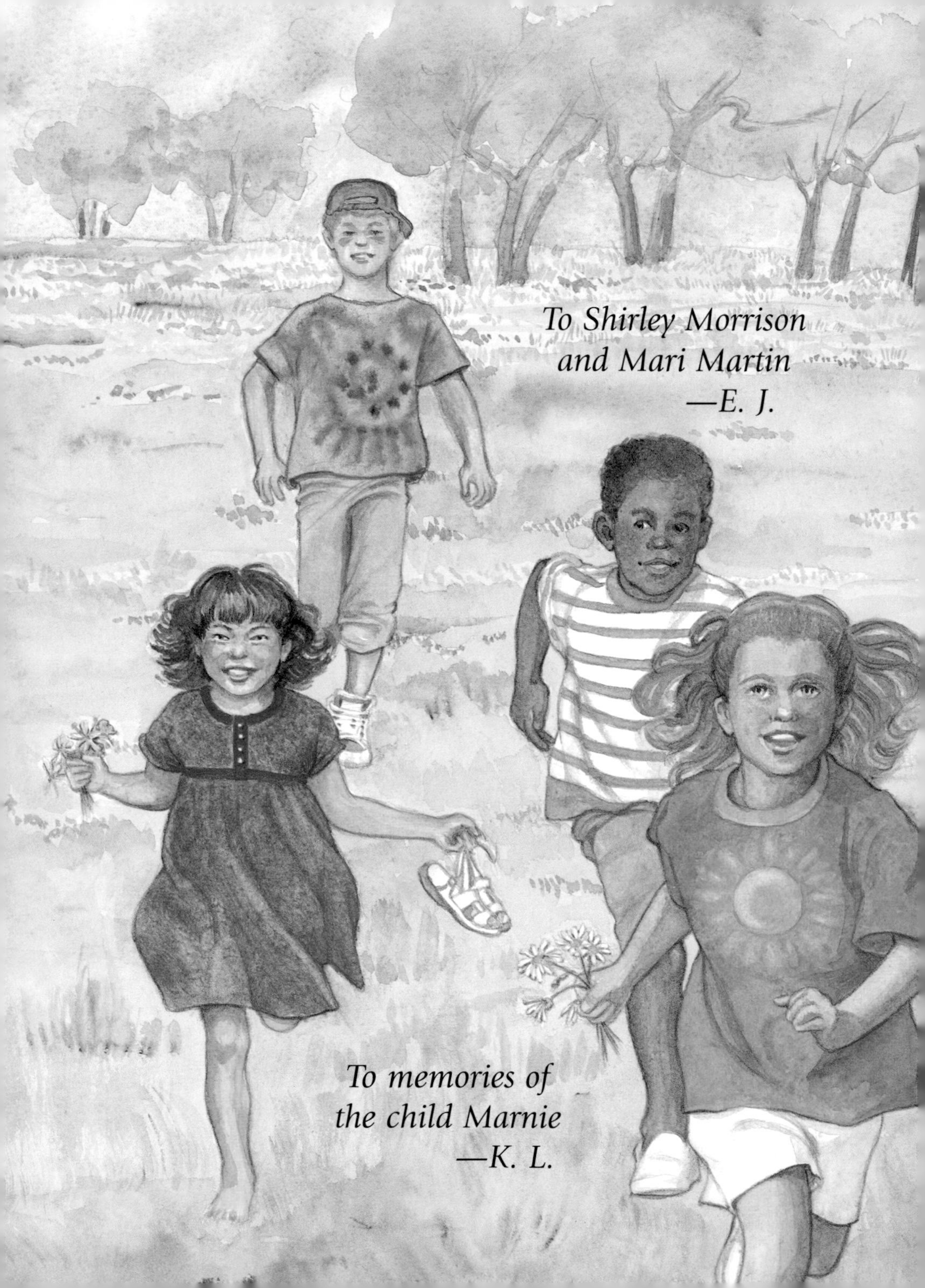

To Shirley Morrison
and Mari Martin
—E. J.

To memories of
the child Marnie
—K. L.

Did You Know?

June is a month of warmth and light. In the Northern Hemisphere, there are more daytime hours in June than in any other month. The morning grass is bright with dew, and evening sunsets linger on the hillsides.

The weather is usually mild and sunny in June. James Russell Lowell, an American poet, wrote, "And what is so rare as a day in June? / Then, if ever, come perfect days."

June smells of new hay and clover, of buttercups and daisies. The trees are fresh with green leaves, and golden columbine blooms in the woodlands.

Several animals and plants take their names from June. The Juneberry is a small, slender tree, and the June bug, also called the June beetle, is a large insect that appears in late spring.

In June, young animals are learning about life. Robins watch their parents search for worms in the grass, and ducklings swim behind their mothers on lakes. Female brown bats carry their babies with them as they fly through the air searching for insects. Wolves teach their young pups to hunt.

June marks the end of school and the start of summer vacation for many children. Some families go camping in the summer. Children look for animal tracks in the mud or hunt for insects under logs. Best of all are the sounds, sights, and smells of the wilderness—the roar of a waterfall, the colors of the wildflowers, or the scent of pine needles.

Children like to play active
games such as Frisbee or tennis in
June. But June is also a good time
to relax with a book in the shade,
enjoy a glass of lemonade, or take
a walk down a country road.

The June Birthstone

June has two birthstones: the pearl and the moonstone. Pearls are found in oyster and clam shells, but you would have to open one thousand shells to find a single natural pearl. Moonstones are gems with silvery spots that glimmer like moonbeams on water. They are found in Sri Lanka and India. For centuries, people believed that the color of moonstones changed as the moon changed its shape in the sky.

The June Flower

If you were born in June, your special flower is the rose. Pictures of roses painted more than three thousand years ago were found in the ancient city of Knossos, Crete. Different varieties of roses are the state flowers of Georgia, Iowa, New York, and North Dakota.

The June Zodiac

Gemini, the twins, is the astrological sign for people with birthdays from May 21 to June 21. People born under Gemini are thought to be bright, interesting, and great company. They like to do three or four things at once. They enjoy learning foreign languages and working with their hands. It is also said that a Gemini is often late to appointments.

The sign for people born from June 22 to July 22 is Cancer, the crab. Those born under Cancer are said to be warm and caring, although sometimes they can be too emotional. They love to be around family and friends and are team players. A Cancer loves food and always has a good appetite.

The Calendar

June is the sixth month of the year and has thirty days. It had only twenty-nine days until the Roman ruler Julius Caesar added a day when he introduced a new calendar in 46 B.C. June marks the beginning of summer in the Northern Hemisphere.

Some historians believe June is named for the Junius family. Members of this family were powerful and important during the early days of ancient Rome. Other historians believe that June is named after Juno, the Roman goddess of marriage, who guided and protected women. This may be why today June is considered the best month for weddings.

Sun, Sky, and Weather

Sunrise comes early in June, creeping over the hills and lighting the trees, the meadows, and the riverbanks. The noon sun is at its highest point in the sky in June. The weather is usually gentle and warm. The soft droning of bees can be heard during the day. In the long evenings, twilight colors fade slowly from gold to pink to purple.

At night, the Big Dipper appears to be standing on its handle. June's full moon has been called the hot moon by some Native American peoples of the Northeast.

Prairie days are warm in June, but the mornings are crisp and clear. By noon, the sun beats down, and animals run for cover. Water oozes from the roots of the prairie grass, keeping the ground damp and cool.

In the desert, June is a harsh month. The temperature may reach one hundred degrees day after day. A hot wind blows, drying up the last traces of spring moisture. The Anglo-Saxons, who settled in Britain in the fifth and sixth centuries, called June *Sera monath*, or dry month.

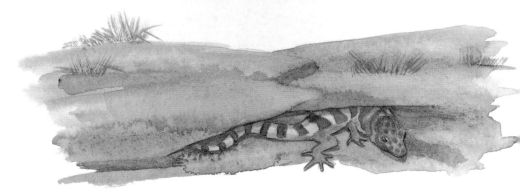

Animals in June

In June, insects are looking for mates. Fireflies twinkle in the woods and meadows. Males and females signal to each other with their lights. In South America, some fireflies flash green and red. Those in North America flash a soft yellow.

Birds sing less often in June than in May. The young have hatched, and the parents are busy caring for them. A brown thrasher, which must feed its young up to six thousand insects a day, does not have time for a song. Neither does the Baltimore oriole, which must bring as many as one hundred caterpillars to its young every hour.

Small birds such as robins, red-winged blackbirds, and kingbirds protect their nestlings by chasing crows away from their neighborhoods. A brave bird might even land on a crow's back and give it a warning peck.

Mammals also protect their young in June. Red foxes will bark at strangers in the woods, giving their pups a chance to escape. Cottontail rabbits, which are usually timid, have been known to attack cats to protect their babies at this time of year.

In the city, June bugs
the size of grapes crash against
window screens. At night, they are
attracted to light. If you let them into the house,
they will fly toward the first lightbulb they see.

Animals in the desert must find ways to stay cool
in June. Desert tortoises have thick shells that give
them some protection. They mate and lay their eggs
in early summer. The sun warms the eggs while the
parents nap in their underground burrows to escape
the heat. Kangaroo rats begin to drool when the
temperature reaches about 107 degrees. This drool
wets their chins and throats and cools them off.
Kangaroo rats never drink water. They get all of their
moisture from the seeds, leaves, and insects they eat.

Plants in June

In the woodlands, roses, chokecherries, and irises are in bloom, and wild strawberries have ripened. Eat a ripe strawberry from the vine and you are in for a treat. They are warm, juicy, and sweet.

The leaves of aspens, poplars, and cottonwood trees rustle in the summer breeze. Seeds from these trees are embedded in cotton fluff. The wind carries them away to distant places. If they land in a place with the right kind of soil and the right amount of moisture and sunlight, they will sprout and take root.

Trees and plants need light in order to grow. Because daylight hours are long in June, many trees grow rapidly during this month. Trees help keep animals and people cool in the summer by providing shade and by returning moisture to the air. On a June day, the average apple tree soaks up ninety-four gallons of water with its roots, but it gives almost all of it back to the environment through tiny pores, or holes, in its leaves.

The Arizona desert is mostly
brown and gray in June, but the
saguaro cactus is green and
blooming. Saguaros often grow
up to fifty feet tall. As many as
one hundred waxy white flowers
may appear on one plant during
its four-week blooming season.
The flowers open between
sunset and midnight and
close the next afternoon.
Because they bloom at
night, the flowers are
pollinated by bats.

Special Days

Flag Day

The American flag is a symbol of the United States, and Flag Day, celebrated each year on June 14, is a time to remember its importance. Flags are flown for many reasons. The flags of an army identify the country for which the army is fighting, and the flag on a ship indicates the ship's place of origin. An old custom is for explorers to plant a flag on new territory to claim it for their country. When American astronauts reached the moon in 1969, they marked the spot with an American flag.

Summer Solstice

The summer solstice occurs around June 21 and marks the first day of summer in the Northern Hemisphere. On this day, the Northern Hemisphere receives more sunlight, and there are more daylight hours than at any other time of the year.

The position of the earth in relation to the sun causes the summer solstice. You can show this relationship with a toothpick, an orange, and a flashlight.

Stick the toothpick in the top of the orange to represent the North Pole. Shine the flashlight, which represents the sun, on the orange, and tilt the North Pole slightly toward the flashlight. You will see that most of the light shines on the top part of the orange. This is the position of the Northern Hemisphere on the summer solstice.

Father's Day

Father's Day is always celebrated on the third Sunday of June in the United States and Canada. Father's Day is a day for people to show love, respect, and appreciation for their fathers, or for someone who has acted as a father to them.

Father's Day was first observed on June 19, 1910, in Spokane, Washington, when Mrs. Sonora Smart Dodd asked the mayor to set aside a day for people to honor their fathers. Later President Calvin Coolidge supported the idea of the holiday. In 1966, Lyndon B. Johnson made Father's Day a national holiday in the United States by presidential proclamation.

Famous June Events

On June 15, 1215, English barons forced
King John of England to sign the Magna
Carta. This document gave important rights
to English nobles and became a part of
English law. The constitutions of the United
States and Canada are based on these rights.
The modern idea of trial by jury comes from
the Magna Carta.

On June 30, 1908, a huge explosion occurred five miles above the earth's surface over Siberia in northern Russia. A long, flaming object was seen flying through the sky just before the blast. Thousands of acres of forest burst into flame, trees were flattened, and many herds of reindeer were killed. Many scientists think that this disaster was caused by a fragment from a comet that heated up and exploded when it entered the earth's atmosphere. It is said to have been the most powerful explosion in recorded history.

On June 18, 1983, Sally Ride began a six-day flight with five other astronauts on the space shuttle *Challenger*. Sally Ride was the first American woman in outer space. During the mission, she helped to conduct scientific experiments and helped to place two communications satellites in orbit.

Birthdays

Many famous people were born in June.

Award-winning children's book author and illustrator, best known for *Where the Wild Things Are*.

Known for the diary she kept while she and her family hid from the Nazis during World War II.

Russian composer and author. Two of his most famous compositions are *The Firebird* and *The Rite of Spring*.

Singer, songwriter, and former member of the Beatles.

Lou Gehrig

June 19, 1903

Baseball player who played in 2,130 consecutive games for the New York Yankees between 1925 and 1939.

Clarence Thomas

June 23, 1948

Judge appointed associate justice of the Supreme Court in 1991.

Jack Dempsey

June 24, 1895

World heavyweight boxing champion, 1919–1926.

Pearl S. Buck

June 26, 1892

Author, authority on China, and winner of the Pulitzer Prize for *The Good Earth* in 1932 and the Nobel Prize for Literature in 1938.

Helen Keller

June 27, 1880

American advocate for the blind and writer, who was blind and deaf from early childhood.

Peter Paul Rubens

June 28, 1577

Flemish painter and diplomat. Two of his most famous paintings are *The Raising of the Cross* and *Helen Fourment and Her Children*.

A June Story

When the world was new, six suns blazed in the sky. The heat was so intense that the land below was scorched and barren.

Finally, the people could stand no more. The emperor of China called his greatest archer, Prince Howee, to shoot the extra suns out of the sky. Prince Howee knew that he could not shoot the suns. They were too far away. But as he cast his eyes down, he saw six golden images reflected in a nearby pool. Drawing his bow, the prince shot the reflections. Soon five of the suns had vanished, and only one remained.

When the last sun saw what had happened to its brothers, it ran and hid behind a mountain. The people called and called, but the sixth sun refused to show its face. The world soon became cold and dark.

"Can no one coax the sun from its hiding place?" cried the emperor.

The wise men called for a tiger. The tiger roared and roared.

"I don't like that noise," said the sun. "And I won't come out."

The wise men called for a cow. The cow lowed softly.

"That's better," said the sun. "But I still won't come out."

At last they brought a rooster.

"Cock-a-doodle-doo," crowed the rooster.

"What a beautiful sound," said the sun. He floated up over the mountain. All the people cheered. The emperor made a little red crown and put it on the head of the rooster. From that day to this, the rooster calls out to the sun each and every morning.

AUTHOR'S NOTE

This book gives an overview of the month of June. But nature does not follow a strict schedule. The mating and migration of animals, the blooming of plants, and other natural events vary from year to year, or occur earlier or later in different places.

The zodiac sections of this book are included just for fun as part of the folklore of the month and should not be taken as accurate descriptions of any real people.

The June story was adapted from *Favorite Children's Stories from China and Tibet* by Lotta Carswell Hume. (Tokyo: Charles E. Tuttle Co., 1962.)

Text copyright © 2002 by Ellen Jackson
Illustrations copyright © 2002 by Kay Life
All rights reserved, including the right of
  reproduction in whole or in part in any form.

Published by Charlesbridge Publishing
85 Main Street, Watertown, MA 02472
(617) 926-0329
www.charlesbridge.com

Illustrations done in watercolor on Fabriano
  hot-press paper
Display type and text type set in Giovanni
Color separations made by Sung In Printing,
  South Korea
Printed and bound by Sung In Printing,
  South Korea
Production supervision by Brian G. Walker
Designed by Diane M. Earley

Library of Congress
Cataloging-in-Publication Data

Jackson, Ellen B., 1943-
    June/Ellen Jackson; illustrated by Kay Life.
      p. cm.—(It happens in the month of)
    ISBN 0-88106-919-1 (hardcover)
    1. June (Month)—Folklore. 2. June
    (Month)—Juvenile literature. [1. June
    (Month)] I. Life, Kay, ill. II. Title.

GR930.J336   2002
398'.33—dc21   2001028267

Printed in South Korea
10 9 8 7 6 5 4 3 2 1